I SHIMMER
SOMETIMES,
TOO

I SHIMMER SOMETIMES, TOO

poems by

Porsha Olayiwola

◇

Published by Button Poetry / Exploding Pinecone Press

Minneapolis, MN 55403 | http://www.buttonpoetry.com

◇

CONTENTS

for the love of self
for the god in me

HAD MY PARENTS NOT BEEN SEPARATED AFTER MY FATHER'S TRAFFIC STOP, ARREST, AND DEPORTATION FROM THE UNITED STATES OF AMERICA

we might all be sitting about the pink kitchen table with the white legs. my father, a taxi driver, might have come home late in the evening with two large chuck steaks bloodied, red, fresh, best he could bring. he might have seasoned the meat, his thick brown hands gently letting loose salt how god did earth. he might lay a sheet of cayenne over the flesh—a homeland conquered by sun, a fire gouged between cheeks, eyes watering a flag of surrender. my father might have survived the night to serve us.

my father, with his skin shiny, his head smooth, might have built me a treehouse in the front yard, with tools from his orange metal box. and my mother, sharp, discerning, the quiet keeper of sacred emblems, our family's marrow, might have never let me climb in that tree house because as it were, gunshots littered our streets the way the dead plague a hospital.

had my father not been deported, he and my mother might have had another child. it's likely they'd build a new back porch and have a garden with peppers just like our neighbor, ronny. my mother might grow a row of cabbage, all green and light, tight and balled like fists. it'd be a wednesday and my father, my brother and i might whisk our bikes down lake shore drive or pitch a tent in the back yard or watch terminator or the movies where eddie murphy played a cop from beverly hills. my father may have been filled with enough cracks in his face to cause an earthquake of laughter to ripple through our home.

dusk, with the light gleaming in from our living room windows, i imagine he might step into one of my mother's bright silk dresses. the purple one. he'd squeeze his feet into her pumps and prance around the house he bought her as a gift years before. my mother might have giggled at my father's silliness. he may have sauntered over to her with his palm down and his wrist bent as though he was expecting to have his hand captured by a long-awaited love.

my mother might have said something like, *man, if you don't take off my good dress, you finna buy me another one.* and my mother may have not really been mad. and you could tell by how she cocked her neck back and to the side, alabaster gleaming a curve into her face. she might have smiled through the threat and my father might have held her around the waist with one arm and pulled her into his chest, how i do the woman i love when i miss her so much it aches.

and my parents may have kissed, maybe on the lips, and my father, full, may have reached his hand to my mother's string of beads, removed it, and placed the necklace over his own head to lay along his chest. her earrings may dance from his lobe. and my father, a man who gave like a tree, might have lined his fingers over my mother's tombed heart and swayed his hips to its cadence.

CONTINENT

from the latin continēre meaning to contain

an island vast
pangea drifting a land mass   beyond
it is soil to be conquered
hadn't it already been

a shore anxious for the ocean
a horizon as gilded partition

what is a continent apart from separation?
a fence in which i peer through voids

a place afar
i know not how to extend my frame

a bed
            for a daughter
a tomb
            for a father
waves and
waves and
waves

away

SOUTHSIDE APOCALYPSE

i don't remember when it started. perhaps
around the same time the homes grew
into shadows boarded and decorned
wooden with brown grass grown over.

or perhaps it was when the butter-burnt pit bulls
took the streets, guarded the avenues like militia,
teeth razored enough to devour a toddler as snack.
the gunshots rang a riddled soundtrack,

a drowned train peppering us, and mikneah
and i knew we were poor, black, not dead yet.
i didn't mind the crouching if it meant chalked
hopscotch tomorrow, or the penny candy store

before school, or church friday night. i recall the day
foggy. we on the other side of pavement at tiffany's.
and the boys would come, armored in shirts draping
to their knees, reminiscent of their mamas in house

dresses. the boys ravished the blocks between 79th
and 87th, scrounging for food or teen girls, a body
to sacrifice, kin to belong to, love or blood,
and that is where i came in. initiation into the GDs

required proof you were inhuman,
and i am a ritualistic offering. skin so
black i'm blue, belly so full i'm gag,
girl convenient with holes, a meal to fill

the boys until the next moon. mikneah's words
chased after each other, her voice more plea
than warning. *there they go,* and i heed, scurry
down basement steps of a vacant building. watch

with my eyes peering over the ledge. hands clasping
concrete. body—compressed stiff. breath—
a hushed prayer to live.

INTERLUDE AT A NEIGHBORHOOD
GAS STATION: 2001

the music peeled back the air
as the ivory chrysler swerved and jolted
into a spot behind our parked toyota.

he gets out the car, slams the door,
say, *shawty, you thick as hell*
i know you out here belonging to somebody
looking how you look.

my sister, skin dark and glittering like oil sheen on black pressed hair,
arches into a smile.
he strides over as if the center of him is being pulled
    toward
    the gravel
    by a slow
    song or
    sweet spirit.

his shorts are low to his ankles, his sweater is large
with COOGI spread 'cross it like love on clean sheets.

i bend my head under and out the window,
fastened on my older sister,
her knuckles shining on her hips,
nails neon and glowing too,

say, *why?*
                        you trying to bag?

she eyeing his car like it's a slice of cake frosted
in a pink swirled dress. my sister drags her tongue
along her lillied lips, grabs the stranger's palm,
and scriptures her digits.

he go into a backward twirl and stroll to his car.
she takes the pump out and closes the cap.
me, curious and peering, seeing a god summon a man,

he drives,
stops,
reverses as though he forgot his house keys
or his wallet or something that belonged to him,

says,
                              ah, pretty girl,
what they call you?

my sister, a hurricane to a puddle,
the north star niggas follow,
say,

                                        patrice.

GOD IS GOOD ALL THE TIME

and all the time

god good

god all good

god all the good

god all the good

all the time
the good is god
and the god is the good
the time god ain't

good is the time

god ain't

god ain't on time

all the time

god ain't good

all the time

god ain't god
all the time
god ain't good
god aint god
all the good aint god

all the time

all the good aint god

all the good is the good

and all the time

that aint god
sometimes is you
sometimes you is god
the good god is you
all good all god

all the time

is you

FOOTNOTES

on coming of age poor, girl, and black on the southside of chicago[1]

change your morning and evening route   every day
                                                                              of every week
                                                                              of every corner
you turn—someone may be a lurking shadow in the margins

know the proper way to dodge bullets: run in a zig zag and not a straight
line bullets shoot straight   you

                                                    zig

                              zag
quickduckdownlaydownstaydowngetonthefloorgetonthefloor

you need to know to run from dogs[2] jump to the hood of a car

carry pepper spray

don't play in the front yard. don't sit on the front porch[3]

do not talk to strangers

talk to some strangers—you need hood allies when the wrong time knock
down your screen door with a warrant like that time Ms. Dee house al-
most got robbed but Bug, off 84th, told his niggas to avoid her house
cause she gave him greens every time they grew in her yard

not everyone survives the summer[4]

smile when a man on the street say smile

---

1. *or, home taught me to run*

2. running from dogs is not the same as running from bullets

3. rashad and i saw a man fire a pistol toward the sky—the bullets flew straight up

4.

smile

come straight[5] home after school

don't let nobody in your mama house when your mama ain't in her house. don't open the door for nobody! not even your mama

if you let somebody beat you, your mother will beat you

also don't fight

fly

also don't yell help   yell fire

also dodge   also bob   also weave

also   flee   run

                                                              run
                              run

---

5. like a bullet

GHAZAL FOR THE CHICAGO TWO-STEP

the only dance i know to make you want to step
into yourself is the chicago-style two-step.

footing matronizes any soggy tune. the
heel heals every duet unfit, unsure. few step

like my aunt. she cut a carpet clean. every brown
liquor shot bring her closer to herself. true step

ever witness an unbroken population
glide, move a wreckage of cartilage break through step,

an exodus on beat so black the sway a great
migration—a flock in every city new step,

clasped hands, red silk hum, two pairs, six count beat, side to
front, dip low back leg cross; who taught you how to step,

young carcass? aging spirit ancestoring the
home you come from insoles, rich with it—make-do step

like love in its name, like swag in vain; scented round
a candied collar, new vest, orange suede shoes step

in my kitchen, i cook, coast, coax the woman i
adore to shimmy, to split wide with me, two-step.

ELLA: @ THE SKATING RINK

& then she says it again
cinderella
as if i didn't hear her screech it the first time
as if i'm not ignoring her high-pitched voice in the first place
& i can see the disco ball illuminating her grim
smirk
cin-der-el-la
so i skate over   slow
wheels turning
& i pop my gum
& i roll my eyes
& i think about how mad i am
my father hid himself 'round in the arms of their mother
& now this goblin and her twin think they some kinda kin to me
cinderella, get over here and tie the laces on my skates
& so at this point
i let   the wheels   roll   me   where   i
need to be
& i think about how she keep calling me |outside of| my name
like my mama ain't already give me my name
keep calling me |outside of| reverence
like my mama ain't dead
like i ain't the last prophecy to come out of a dying god
& i think about my name
how it is the first gift i gift to a stranger
the first thing that was mine i ever gave willingly to the world
how it tumbles up my throat and outside my mouth like a street fight
ready to gut   me   free
& the wheels   they slow
& i feel a thumb onto the platform this goblin is perched up top of
& her teeth have rotted into a shade of red from the lights
& i can smell her skin melting
& i bend down so i can really see her
& i feel her breath, unworthy of existence

& i think about taking off the cap and pouring my soda pop in her hair
but i don't
i look at her   i say
that ain't my name
& i skate   off

THE BUS STOP IS CROWNED MOTIF

i.
the bus stop is often memorial
ground, often a street corner, which is a
waving white flag, a signal to cease. the
headlights shine fright at just the right second

and i count it an urban miracle:
the man has not asked me for something i
will not give, the girls do not want my shoes.
the chase is not for my body: dark, fat,

and queer. those who have the least are often
offered up at a crossroad. those in need
are often slain in the dead of mourning.
those in power smile, name this a just fate.

palms grip to makeshift knives when we travel
as to not be the tale they warned us of.

ii.
as to be neither feared fable nor tale,
we lace keys and pencils in fingers, move
in packs to avenues well lit. we clinch
fare, we do not sit on the bench, we stand.

percy tells me of the time the lady
at the beauty supply store saved his life.
five boys from the high school up the street wanted
what he had and what, i guess, they didn't:

his sneakers, his jacket, his life. either
way, he said he didn't mind fighting if
it meant living. he fell into the store
boned, as one does a sanctuary, when

waiting for god to show mid-plight, patient,
armed and watching for the ride toward home.

iii.
armed and watching for the chariot home,
the shelter is shattered cemetery
of looking glass beneath my feet and i
wonder who was it that came undone here.

i think of sakia, a black girl more
her daddy than her mother. she and the
lord, sky, got the same complexion when she
leave the pier to wait for a bus on a

corner. a man drives by, stops, catcalls, and
don't take lesbian as an answer. does
what any man would do in such a threatening
situation. he grips his knife and it

is her, i know, pooling at my feet, as
i wade in wait for what may never show.

iv.
i wade in weight for what may never show.
i think on how often people who look
this wide, my shade, and squeezed 'tween ma'am and sir
are thrust against curbs, are those closest to

a lineage of death. when two or more
margins meet at an edge, they create a
jagged funeral. take any hood post
of flag or shrine in glory. the difference

is in the length of time the blood has had
to blot. i do not tuck a blade when i
travel to places memories will not
take me. night, prayer, or bodies, i can

hear the surface crack, can hear the bursting
engine sounding toward the memorial.

MY BROTHER GHOST WRITES THIS POEM

the phone clanks its chains | my younger brother is on its other end | the court ruled that he bed at a residence | following release from the county | i hear him hurdle in | hop out his manic | he holy spirit sees my work | says he | got ||| bars ||| too | bellows out if he can write my words | in place of my words

my brother first ghouled | thoughts: hallucinating phantom | government a plot for his plot | he mad mad mad | scientist | on to something fishy swamping in the soda cans | run run run | and we cannot reach | my brother is disappearing | shadow of him | self

and forgets | memories have gravestones | brain has visitors wandering bare corridors | paranormal activity is conjuring family's well kept skeletons | shhh people listening | supernatural | he god | he god | how great is god | praise god | praise allah | made in my brother's image | god is he | and who am i | to not have faith | to not smell magic | shattering i want to tell my mother the exorcisms do not exhort | my brother is | not | possessed | imagination | just fleeing | haunted mansion | depression built | if my brother is ghost then i am banshee | scream of little boys | things lost | if my brother is sick then i am morgue | try to keep | my dead | memories | from spilling | out of | my hands

soon | i will be ghost too | my chemistry will open too | the night will vanish inside my mind too | after my brother reads a poem through the phone | i know that we are both in limbo | teetering too close to lines | i don't tell him i shimmer sometimes too | i only listen | to the static | in the background | sticking out its arm | stretching for my brother | and me too

DYKE PREPARES TO SEE HER FAMILY

i   glide   the   knife   across   my   stomach
                             gut the pot out
                             lay it on my dresser

i find strands from my last haircut on the floor,   in the trash
and i glue them back to my scalp
sit monolithic as it dries

                 i gauge around my blackened knees
                 round the wand into a circumference
                 and tilt so each cap pops, pops out
                  rolls, and lands near my feet

i want to make less of me
packaged enough for the holidays
i pack my bags and board
the three-hour flight to minneapolis
when i land i find privacy
in a single-stall restroom

i plunge my hand past my ribcage
and rip the organ from my chest
my hand throbbing to keep pace

i place my heart in a mason jar
and screw the lid shut
i button my shirt
exit the bathroom

and head down the escalator to my family

blood splatting
between the seams
of the machine as i descend

ODE TO MY EX-GIRLFRIEND

regal god // collarbone as necklace // brown sand shade // the sun's favorite golden offspring // wide smile // short hair // nia long-fine // ode to you // who left me breathless // at the base of a mountain during my most recent asthma attack // whose glasses of wine took to screaming // for me to shut up // as i sat front a room filled // my bed is as lone as silent as the day you ignored me at the eiffel tower // you the only person in the only language i knew // departed

lover // my knowing now is full // as our sink with our dirt // dishes piled like neglect on a worn sweater // as full as liane's car with my clothes, my books, my lamp you claimed and the salvagables i tossed in the back seat // perhaps had it not been for you // sweet ache // i wouldn't have known what it is to feel lonely // next to someone you love // i wouldn't have known alone as the most comforting

demon // i thank you for adoration in its endless state // of a pitiful hanging on // i thank you for never vacating this body // for teaching me forever // does end // if not for you, dearest dweller, i don't know that i would have aged // don't know that i would have lit boxes of cigarettes or started attending therapy

i wish you the same you have managed to gift me // but also healing // the want to live // despite // to pass a photo of me// without pause // to stroll near our old apartment // have it be just a brick building off a main road //

i wish you unlocked doors // meals prepared side by side // i wish you concerts under stars // with someone you love // wish you trips overseas with someone you never want to stop talking to // i wish you trust // after my betrayal // i wish you love after loss //
i wish you love //
after love //
after love

MEMORY / LOSS

when i meet someone   i greet them   with an apology. i've
forgotten   their name. we had met at some time
     in some place   before this.
i tell them "sorry"   i am sure to look at them and not through them
     like   i must have done the last time.   i explain

my bad memory: i forget my family's birthdays.
i don't remember to celebrate
my own.   i can't ever remember anything but a
fading
     face these days.
     recollection
     is a foul
     trick.
one can reimagine the past different than
how it happened.
change the color of your favorite   ball,

switch out the knives
for spoons,

swap out the house for
home,

think the door
was always
falling off its
hinges,

build   a friendship out of someone
     who is not there. i don't remember [people]
     or
     i can't recall the names attached to the people i meet.

my brain places new acquaintances into short   term
[compartments]
as their expected length   of occupancy. my memory
is trying to save me
                        [from remembering]
someone who is not there   after a while [so] after a while,
                        it erases [person]
                        before [person]
                        erases themselves.

"sorry"   i greet people   with apologies. "sorry"

my family, halfway 'cross the   country,

my father,   halfway across   the   world,
the best friends i do not have,

the   woman my heart reminds me to remember to love—
i can't recall if they are the ones who did the leaving or if i was the one who
forgot to show.

maybe when i say   i have a
bad memory
what i mean is
        just that.
                i'm filled on bad memories.

[brain replays the departure]
i, more hollow
i, more abandoned:

                memory works in association.
                you will always associate two together.

maybe my brain can't unwind love from   [   ]

can't dissociate the building of a home from   the breaking

of an entryway.

don't know what it is to get lost   in someone
and not lose
yourself.
falling   [in love]
and falling.

perhaps by not remembering i am protecting myself.
perhaps   forgetting is self-preservation.

when i meet someone, i ask them to tell me their name. i say it aloud
hoping it'll stay, hoping they'll stay.

i can't
recall if
anyone
ever did.

FINDING A BLACK QUEER WOMAN LOVE WITH WHOM YOU ARE COMPATIBLE IS LIKE FINDING A WATERMELON SEED LODGED IN THE PUPIL OF WHOLE FRIED CHICKEN

i will be alone forever   then

and how long is infinity?

does it measure itself in memories or moments?

how many summer camp swing-set weddings does it hold?
how many dinners aside the atlantic does it yield?

does it fossilize the   broken   bones,
frameless   doors,
fractured promises
collapsing like lungs
and longing?

does it stretch past smashed phones
and the lamp we fought one another for?

how many sheer curtains have been torn from their panes
before forever's end is reached?

do we ever arrive?
i suppose not,
and isn't that the jag?
to go unresolved?
unfinished?

                    to push   and give

and   turn   over   all   your   hands   have   learned   to

hold   and   then   to   still   keep
going,
to be limitless in

                              solitude,

to be the void
vast and abyssal,

a great and dark skyline

                              spanning.

TIME CAPSULE

it has taken centuries to arrive
here in the same room. i do not
unlove. that is not the question.
i love everyone i have ever loved

intensely and against time.
all i can remember though,
when i am walking into the lounge,
is the door. she is inside and just

as i have known. except there
is a scarf keeping her hair.
on the right of her face, a curl
escapes to ask if i recall

how she twirled the strand
with her fingers and i know
the resolve viscerally. we go
on here, and like this, for ages:

staring at the other's stare, never
ordering, ordering finally, finally
ordering too many. she is smiling
and i am giddy. my mouth cannot

keep pace with my brain. my opening
is an entry into a lifespan we missed.
we sneak smokes in the bathroom.
all that i say causes her to cry

laughter. we are teenagers or old
friends or old lovers who cannot
unquarrel. it is so easy to relive
and even easier to relive regret.

and now i am thinking of the door
again: why i walked through it,
why i broke the door from its hinges,
how we were naked and yelling,

running about the house, to
and away from each other.
that is the vehicle that delivered
us here. and somehow we have

arrived. apart and whole.

THE JOKE

a dyke walks into a bar and the bartender asks if she wants to lick-her. a dyke walks around in the world and the joke is on her. a dyke comes out the closet and all the mouths cackle. all the hands pick up stones. all the mothers bury their daughters. a dyke does nothing, holds up the wall at a club, and all the femmes still ask this hoe's name. all the straight women lean in. all the lips part singing. a dyke prays in a temple and the sanctuary sprouts eyes and the walls grow teeth. a dyke cracks into a smile on a tv sitcom and doesn't outlive the season finale. a dyke finds solace in another dyke's arms and [just kidding, the joke is still on her]. a dyke stumbles into a white queer party and no one sees her, no one can un-blend nighttime from nigger. a dyke drinks a beer at a gay bar and a man grabs her ass, reminds her that what is hers is not. a dyke brings a date to the family reunion and they both get hung from the family tree. a dyke waits for the bus and [ha ha] never makes it home. a dyke grinds on the dance floor and bullets bring her knees to a buckle and she falls out, dead, with laughter.

I'M THE TYPE OF FANCIFUL WARLOCK WHO COOKS UP IRRATIONAL FEARS IN MY IDLE MIND WITH A CRACK PLASTERED BETWEEN MY CHEEKS.

yo, yo, yo, facts: i am the god of irrational pregnancy scares. check. in the third grade i got detention for throwing wood chips in joel's face cause he kissed me on the goddamn mouth on the playground and i thought this nigga was trying to get me pregnant. check. at summer camp, my counselor made us do these intense push-up cardio jumping jacks and she would be like, *yeah! yeah! you feel that pain? yeah. that's what sex is like!* and then she told this story about this girl who *let* a penis touch her thigh. bruh. the girl never had sex but then got pregnant and i was like, *damn.*

this is like jesus. and somehow i knew from that moment i must be wary of my body and impeding immaculate conception. yo. even. if. i. never. had. sex. in. my. entire. life. i could be pregnant. woke up sick one summer, thought i was pregnant. took too many naps in one week, must be pregnant. the woman i love

       reaches for my hand

on a broad boulevard
and for the first time

i hope there
is a budding.

sometimes when i make love
to a woman and i fill her and feel filled by her, by how she wraps her whole around me, i know we are a warm birthing | a body unsplit | a soft flesh rupturing a new skin | a hot wish | a goodgoodgood dream come flourishing | rest of my nights | plant a future alive | within this woman.

i'm the type of fanciful warlock fairy dyke god who believe in freedom [as love] and [love as] magic so much so i think i could get a woman pregnant if i just placed my all inside. yo. if i tied a kiss to the end of my fingers, maybe it may land in her womb. check. if i cast my heart outside my chest maybe it might pulse a way.

i am the god of irrational pregnancy scares: afraid of what i may never give, afraid of what may never be given. i am terrified of losing a lover: again. afraid this so intersectional, you have to be at exactly the right point in the universe to receive it | comes round once a revolution, bruh | and we can't afford the science, nor the chemistry granted our kind of [love].

sometimes, i joke with my lover

about our good sex | my headboard | my face as her throne. i joke about how *the world does not need little porshas running around putting boogers on people.* i joke of our baby-making music and how it might sing us a chorus nine-months' earshot away from this song. and she laughs at my absurdity | our inability to conceive. sits on my lap. stares into my smile. as though she is expecting something.

TWERK VILLANELLE

for Valentine

my girl positioned for a twerk session—
            knees bent, hands below the thigh, tongue out, head
turned to look at her body's precession.

she in tune. breath in. breasts hang. hips freshen.
            she slow-wine. pulse waistline to a beat bled
for her, un-guilt the knees for the session.

fair saint of vertebrae—backbone blessing,
            her pop-in innate. her pop-out self-bred,
head locked into her holied procession.

dance is proof she loves herself, no questions,
            no music required, no crowd needed.
she arched into a gateway, protecting—

this dance is proof she loves me, no guessing.
            a bronx bedroom, we hip-to-hip threaded.
she turn to me, tranced by her possessing.

she coils herself to, calls forth a legend—
round bodied booty, bounce a praise ballad.
she break hold, turn whole in a twerk session.
body charmed, spell-bent, toward progressing.

LISTEN: MY RIGHT HAND IS COVERED IN BLOOD

we are in my bed again and i am holding
her. this is unlike how we usually fuck. her
spine is nested along my forearm and her
hands lace my neck. everything is gentle.
the lyrics blare for us to bend back and hair
tangles the birth of her name in my mouth.
i love her hair. black, big, uncoiling as we
thrust. my thighs pillow the vibrator pressed
to my clit. this more than the love fabled to
us as children. back to the blood though. it
is what makes me cum. listen: sometimes
i want to get closer than what is physically
possible and entering is the only way to
vanish the distance of our bodies. i feel wet
slick sliding. she opens and gives. what she
keeps inside is now outside for me, wrap-
ping around my wrist, scarlet bracelet, band
of fluid too thick, i ravel and ravel and ravel
and she apologizes for the blood. i tell her i
am grateful for the scent of ore rolling over,
for my hands bursting cherries, for palms
that bloom roses at her call.

I WISH TO EAT WHAT MY PARTNER DOES NOT
AND THIS IS HOW WE LOVE

i want to gobble up

my sweetie pie, a divine ass

plated. i salivate,

i want to lick her legs

thighs & breast cantaloping

secretion seeds, swallowed all

she is clean & devoured,

banquet the bedroom. burst

the seams of her throat,

i glutton lust my sugar plum.

keep the bones, slim relic

heave into her arms,

satiate my sap-tooth,

my girlfriend, cautious lover

of food, sees me lie

stuffed full from meat

oiled in my mouth. bulging gut

for her to feast upon.

i am splayed & uneaten,

lard meal. we purge the night

away. she can't fit me inside

stomach retch at the site.

cake-pop waste the flesh

for the love of feeling famished

probe me with the fork,

spew the fattened darling

all over the satin sheets.

TO DISTINGUISH AN ELEPHANT FROM A HUSKY BLACK GIRL, ONE MUST LOOK CLOSELY AT THE WREATHING OF THE NOOSE

Circus elephant Murderous Mary was executed in Unicoi County, Tennessee, where a crowd of more than 2,500 people looked on, September 13, 1916.

the most alluring circus attraction was a girl.
let any strange man mount & parade porsha
down the town's main road. let the masses wide
gawk & shove peanuts in the girl's erupting jaw.
attempt to hang the circus girl & the crane snaps.
the girl falls. her hips pop from the weight.

> an elephant took a date to the carnival but the lap-bar
> wouldn't lay level along her stomach. she is the reason
> the spin hasn't spun, why the joy rots the air, why the elephant
> & the elephant's lover smack on salmon-colored cotton candy
> until their taste buds flicker numb like festive lights.

the circus girl & the elephant are both empty
of empty, are both full & fool & found
easily, are the fattest lynching,
are both metaphor & both not
slim enough to fit.

> the bumper cars are the single carnival
> attraction able to hold the elephant & so
> the elephant rides round the looped lanes.

during the second attempt, the crowd cheers when
the crane raises the circus porsha from the dirt.
the children swell ecstatic. for the beast with its minstrel
heart has been splayed. and this is the most magnificent
show / the one we've all been

> dying for.

URSULA :: HOTEL POOLSIDE

it was fun but this here is how i enjoy my vacation best :: poolside :: laying
out like a pancake on a hunter's early platter :: letting the sun gobble me
dark despite :: what my mama say about it rotting my skin

in its stomach :: i got my book ::
    a bathing suit :: that's tight but
    not enough :: to offend a body
    :: i take a sip of my drink :: bite
    into a shrimp

gluttonous :: i'm still waiting for sheena to come down from the room ::
                    where she at any way :: girl as slow as a state tax
                    refund :: then she got the kinda limbs that have the
                    right to be frantic

i ate half the shrimp and :: most of the olives :: she gon' be mad i ain't
                            under :: a tree and she subject to
                            getting darker :: god forbid the
                            night :: god forbid she dark enough
                            to what :: look like me :: i walk to
                            the edge

of the swimming pool and plop :: on top of the no-diving sign :: the sun is
savage :: salivating all over my chest :: i need to get in water :: that's where
i feel whole :: where the boy on deck can't insult :: my form with his eyes ::
i need to be baptized under :: my own god :: i get close to the ledge :: i ain't
illiterate so i jump :: not dive :: the ripples chase each other :: and a god
wash over me :: feel like i'm a luxury :: i am under :: water moving :: body
gray hippopotamus graceful :: i stay :: as long as my lungs allow :: i hear

ewwww :: snub boy complaining to his mama :: the fat girl :: the
                    black killa whale :: and i remember why i can't
                    stand :: white kids :: he the type my limbs slither
                    to squeeze :: what he says reminds me :: of my

mother and what she say :: about my rumble
thighs :: reminds me

of the dressing rooms :: in clothing stores i don't fit :: pants
tailored :: to strangle :: joy :: he
reminds me

of an uncle :: who says *you've gotten big* in place of *hello* :: and i start to think
of eighth grade snowballs thrown :: at a target practice hard to miss i think ::
of the eyes refusing me in the club and :: the seatbelt on the flight here :: or
the fucking band on the roller coaster

and it's like :: shit :: people constructed the whole ::
fat :: world with the
intention i wouldn't
survive it

i think of my arms :: bodies in themselves :: reaching
for the boy calling me free :: willie :: of my vacation
being sucked out like flesh from faulty marrow :: of
me giving the world what they want :: a death match ::
then sheena :: zeus to poseidon :: come on deck :: she
got a

caramel glow :: a wrist slim :: model-fine features :: bikini more worried about
its place in a chiquita banana music
video than being offensive :: her
skin :: flexing with sunscreen :: her
hair :: all diasporic curls :: she
walks

over to me and says :: *ursula* :: *what you think about my swimsuit* :: *does it
make me look fat* and i :: think what you mean :: fat like a whale or fat like
me :: i take a shallow breath :: swallow the watermelon fixed in my trachea
and say :: *nah* :: *girl you look* :: *good now come on* :: *dang*

NOTORIOUS

after i read, the boy with the long, blonde, shaggy ponytail says, "your set was great, like, don't be offended when i say this but, you remind me of biggie smalls."

if i shouldn't be offended | why do you say something you believe | has a chance of offending me | offend | meaning to hit | strike | against | when you say offend | do you mean the blackness is the strike | or the fatness is against me

|

he says this and | i become who he believes i am | my hands thicken | my fingers plump | my long twists shrivel into a short afro | my chin oceans a shadow | my cheeks tumor typhoons | my lips are fat pink | each | word | drags | itself | out | my | mouth | like a guarded hearse | each line | break | squeezes a song | a rap | a dance | beat for this boy tonight

|

biggie smalls | and i are both geminis | we are both twins | of each other | we both tar | dark | thick | it's a wonder | how we heave | and heave | and weave | and stand | behind a mic at all | we all | black and ugly as ever | however we spell well | B | I | G | all rhyme and good time | we both love it when you drive by | and call us | big | poppa | ain't you ever been popped off | been shot at | been blown up like the world trade | don't you like your meat center medium | brown skin rift | red nectar running off the curb of the plate

|

the difference between a fat black nigga rapping and a fat black dyke po-eming is in the cadence of the eulogy spit | or | the difference between a fat black nigga rapping and a fat black dyke poeming is in the faith of the women who love to love us back

|

it is september 2016 | i am on a stage in texas reading poems outdoors | perspiration jogs from my tight curls and finds shelter along my lips | my underarms are a swamp | and still | i do a rap i wrote | and they laugh | de-spite the heat they sing along | arms reach up | in surrender | i am a secu-lar god | a holy holy | words jetting out like jamboree | and i worry | i look too much like | a concert | like black joy leaping | like a hip-hop song in the 80s | a house party walled in saturation | like summertime | like somebody | everybody | wanna be a part of | like a sweet jam sweatin | blasting | juicy

BRUNCH WITH TWELVE BLACK PHANTOMS

CHARACTERS:

MALCOLM X
BIGGIE SMALLS, *aka big poppa*
CLEO, *from set it off*
AUNT JEMIMA
AALIYAH
MUFASA, *king of pride lands, simba's father*
DARREN, *the teen intern from the museum of science and industry who got shot the summer before he started his full-ride at northwestern*
REKIA BOYD
WHITNEY HOUSTON, *icon*
AUDRE LORDE
JAMES BALDWIN, *black expatriate*

	darren ◇	◇ malcolm x	
mufasa			aaliyah
	SEATING CHART		
aunt jemima			biggie smalls
whitney houston ◇		◇ cleo	

SETTING:
the play takes place at malcolm's house on summer sunday near noon in the after afterlife. the air is thick and hot and you can hear someone's mother yelling for you to stay out of the sun.

("stay outta the sun, stay outta the sun" is a mantra echoed through the duration of the play)

the table is long and wooden with an off-white lace tablecloth curving at both sides. it's set underneath a yellow canopy off a sodden pond. the grass is mowed and the cotton is flying high in a field to the left. trimmed sunflowers stand in two large mason jars at both ends of the table. in the center lie platters of food: vegan mac and cheese, fresh chitterlings, fried chicken, baked chicken, barbecued chicken, gluten-free cornbread, collards, sweet potatoes glazed with honey and roasted caramel brown with marshmallows, burnt slightly like a hungman from a willow.

the chairs all hold a body upright with the exception of four ghostless spaces in the center. the open pairs stare across at one another.

(the sun positions itself high and the stage is illuminated a golden yellow)

LORDE: (heard off stage) i keep telling this fool, i ain't afraid. fear is a stranger same way jesus been. and what i got to keep silent for. silence ain't never saved no one. who? show me a quiet stance and i'll show you a grave.

(enter JAMES BALDWIN & AUDRE LORDE, arm in arm, cackling with cigarettes in their mouths)

act one, scene one

TODAY IS A DAY OF TINY MASSACRES

wherein the flight attendant laughs about my name, or i am pulled over
on my way home from tour, or the european foreigner ask me where to
buy drugs at the bar

and so, before i leave my home, i remove my skin

i pull the nude   zipper
                      from
                      under
                      my
                      chin
                      down to my waist.

                i reach to my shoulder and peel   back
                        the   dark
                        bark   brown
        coating.

i pull the sheath to my knees and step
out of
                          my skin

like it is a jumpsuit
                          i spent too much time
letting the outside get on, i hang my skin

over the arms of my chair like a leather jacket,

wrinkles, a rippled heirloom

(de) faced myself in

the mirror

this flesh,   all veins and   blood and

```
        meat              animal
            large                    eyes sphere stare
                                             back
black

                                         blooming
pink
salmon
budding         bright        red          lines    running
                                                     all    over
                                                     my    body
                                                     like   soldiers.
```

ODE TO MOUTH

mouth a basket

        mouth   give   give   give

mouth eager   mouth silent

        mouth a river, a lake

             say *gimme what mine is*

mouth a house

    house got a family of eight who like to stay up late and talk shit

mouth play dominoes   mouth a curse   mouth a pray

mouth come from my mama mouth   my mama mouth big
mama mouth don't stop moving   mama mouth run off
        mouth hungry

        got teeth   mouth eat
mouth black
mouth dark
got a regurgitating history

        mouth heard too much

now it dont know how to shut itself

        mouth wide
        mouth a train
        mouth coming

for who coming

mouth say you can't have all this gutter

        all this non-publishable

mouth say *so*
say *so*
so
so

so

mouth say *salt*

say *salt*

mouth a rifle

mouth   bang

bang

mouth cool

mouth got cool words falling out itself and landing in white people's
          cheeks

mouth on fleek

     mouth hip

mouth finessed

million dollar mouth

mind yourn stay outside of my mouth

mouth dig

you a place to lay

mouth bury you sweet sugar cane

mouth hold you tight

wrap   you   around   its   smut

mouth squeeze

mouth choke

mouth   fat   hole

swallow   you

swallow   you

swallow   you

swallow   you

swallow   you

swallow   you

TANGLED A.K.A
RAPUNZEL A.K.A. LONG-
HAIR-DON'T-CARE AND WHAT

I'm standing in the checkout line at the grocery store, been standing, waiting, patiently. At least I ain't busted. My hair is laid and I got these freshies on my feet, so at the minimum, if I'm out here for this long, I give the people something kind to look at. My sister say don't matter if the lights are cut off at the crib or uncle take over your bed and you don't have a place to sleep, stay dressed to impress. In other words, stay fly. Say you never know who you gon' see out here in these streets.

And I'm thinking, I might see the whole damn city here cause for a reason unknown to me they only have one register open tonight. I open up my flaming hots to curb my hunger. I'm too ready to get back to the high rise at Cabrini. Anyway, it's my turn, and I start loading my groceries onto the moving conveyor belt at the counter.

I see the cashier, scanning, all frantic and shit. Then he takes the time to look up at me, you know, like I'm a person or whatever. He says, *Wow, I really love your hair, it's beautiful.* And I think bout time cause I knew I was looking like a bag of money, bout time someone noticed all this fine, bout time I get ready to say thank you, this freckled-face redhead says, *If you don't mind me asking—is it yours? Is it weave? Can I touch it?* And then this pumpkin-looking motherfucker is no longer touching my groceries but has his crusty pale sore fingers in my hair. And I don't say anything. Which is crazy

cause I'm known to cut a bitch quick for just looking at me too long in the projects. But here, I feel stiff, like a brick high-rise building or a redwood coffin, like the black dress they buried my mother in, like my brother

and all I can think about is death.

I can feel his fingers in my hair, but I think I'm dead. And I wonder if I ever belonged to me anyway. I wonder if I am just a beautiful thing meant for

the world to make theirs. I think about how I gave myself something kind
to look at in this ugly world and now he gone go and touch it and make it
his too. I think I must not belong to me—I'm his too. He touch the whole
world and it's his too.

I wish I was kin to Medusa right now, that my hair would grow
heads and bite his fingers bloody and he would jerk back his
hand. I wish my hair could morph into knives, switchblades
or machetes. I wish each strand was a rope so I could hang
each of his fingers to death. Levitate his hands from my scalp.

Don't he know my scalp
is holy ground. My hair
is black magik. I think
I put a spell on you,

White Boy, I scream
to no one as I hand
him the money.

BLACK BODY WALKS TO THE CORNER STORE IN 13,839 PIECES

and   the   black   body   can't   keep   itself   together
           it   bends   the   corner   and   a   portion of
itself   brushes   a   fence

                                        crumbles
the body   tries to catch   itself   in   quaking palms
pieces sizzle to the concrete

                             in an attempt to clasp itself
the body tilts forward

                             stumbles into a jog happenchance

its knees giving way to   flying   fractures

                             its legs ruptured towers
the body catches itself
               rises   and   steps   forward
                             raining fragments   as it meets pavement
it climbs up to the store

uses   what   is   left   of   itself   to   reach   for
the   handle
its right hand filled with its heart
its legs
hairs
cheeks where the body's mother may have once kissed
elbow
knuckles
spilt
a customer pushes the door on his way out
                                and the door slams into the black body
shattering   it   horizontally
a scattering sprayed on the sidewalk
before the body could ever even purchase its pack of newports

I MILLY ROCK ON ANY BLOCK

i know not where you lie in the great hall
of black boogie-down moves,
yet i know you are glorious, legendary.

i dare not call you a dance—
you ain't no mash potato,
no heel-toe nor shuffle shuck, no jive.

you summertime freedom,

the emblem of any turn up
two times at the club,
one time with dj whysham at the house
got my mama and her friends at the backyard bbq.

we open-palmed procession
taking in of god's favor,

a step from right
to left then side
to side then right
into the fullness
of me. make me
praise me, an orbit
round my chest.

you sugar-talk me into taking space,
you love hard edge swipe move stomp side,

you are neither soft nor delicate.
you are the last part of any city to be gentrified,
the blackest of black

movement, an indication of fight
survival perpetuated, it becomes rhythm
no one can conjure.
you are a battle drumming through my body,

                                          arms reaching,
waving.

you tell me the land is mine
even if it is stolen,

                              even if the ground is bedazzled in my blood
i should wield my anger shiny,

forge each limb into the branch of my body's army,

ready to riot,
ready to dance,
and they will never think to see

us coming.

(AGAIN)

i thought we might have been speeding across the delaware bridge. i pictured myself prying down the windows of his blue sports car and wiggling my far-ranged hips through the porthole as the water rushed inside. but once i made it safely out, I realized I had panicked (again).

maybe febo wasn't driving fast. (perhaps) my mind was moving fast (again). or was it the weed? i was buzzed so i relaxed, turned up the music, and sang into the wind. i didn't hear the sirens call out to me by name. i didn't feel. we had slowed to a stop. and here we were

halted in the fork of a sterile highway. i turned to febo and hear his eyes apologize. the air around us is a myth of good good bud and my shoulders atone for the stench. i looked at febo's creamed skin, down to my dark knees, and then out

to the side view of objects in the mirror glistening closer than they appear. the car door slammed and the sound of the hooves were (faster or) louder or closer. my palms were a pond; mouth a caked land. how does one run when one is fastened?

what glass might i shatter to survive? the officer walked to my window, bent over and into the vehicle, and i feel his breath running its hand along my cheek. his hairs tickling my face (and i am ready). i turn right to greet the police. i stare in two dark

tunnels for nostrils and he snorts. the officer's pink mouth squeals wide. two hooves hang over the inside of the car. i relax (again). it is only a pig. i look at febo and he laughs. and so does the hog (again) and somehow, my guilt giggle gets choked in my throat (like i'm drowning) and as i

am watching myself die in my mind (again), the officer places his front legs on the ground, oinks, and walks back to the marked car. his backside, a coiled emblem springing good goodbye, a shriek of not this time. his tail, an end circling back on itself, a squeal heard over and over

(again).

AFTER JAMES BROWN

          say it!

                 say it!

                      say it loud!

say, *black*

say it,

say it loud, i'm black & i'm proud

say it

say it

sang it

saaaaang it

say it proud!

say it loud!

say it *black*!

black! look-a here

it!

it! say *black*

say it! black!

say *i black*

it black

i black

it black

i black

uh, alright now

say it   say it   sang *it*   say *it*

say it proud!

say it loud!

say it black!

black-it!

black-it proud!

black-it loud

say it loud!
i'm black
it black
i'm black,
it black
it loud
good god, it loud!
say *it loud & black*
say *it loud & it black*
say *i'm black & i'm loud*
good god

say it back!
say it black! black
say it proud! black!
say it proud black!
proud black!
black
say it loud black!
say it black
say it back
look-a here
say it

         sang it
       saaaaang it
    say im black. im loud
     say it, good god
        say it
     sang it (ha ha ha)
        sang it
      lord-a, lord-a

BLACK SPELLS cross a cursed atlantic/ *blacks sail*/ tight packed/
bodies stacked/ bruised backs below/ chains lock/ ship rocks/ bile
moves/ piss splash/ mother raped /her son dead/he bled/captain lost/
five hunnid per head/ slave trade

black sales/stand top/ auction block/ three feet high/still low/ head
straight/hands up/shirt off/pants down/ bend over/turn around/ nigger
boy / age forty/now sold/freedom stole/ caged in

black's cell/ six feet by eight feet/boxed in/defeat/ cops took/ nightstick
to beat/ to knees/one third/ black men/ will live/ closed in /private pris-
ons/his time for his dime/ squirmed like S behind bars/dollar signs

black sells like   aunt jemima hotcakes   stacks sell like

white miley bent to make it shake/   twerk miley/

     crack sells   like

tims and rims and white women   who trade black dresses in
for orange jumpsuits/

  course katie got cornrows   cause plaits sell

like *blacks sail*

     like ships   carry
  captured cargo

   'cross   cursed
   seas

     like concrete   carry
  captured men

shells in cursed cells

slave auction sales/stolen

                                                            culture

                                                                sells

uncle sam sells   sailed niggers   by the seashore   niggas who fail

                              to be sold at sale
                              centuries later end in cells

not enough   sells

                to make jail bail
dwell

                                        on tipped
                                        scales

cells still swell   & you can   still tell a tale   about a
sale

            one made off

                                      a nigga

UN-NAMED

after the civil war, recently-freed slaves took a last name like freed-
men or freeman. others took the last name of their slavemaster. some
because they had to swiftly give a name to their newly acquired citizen-
ship. others with the hopes that they might be reunited with family who
had been sold or separated during the institution of slavery.

my mother's maiden name is battie, spelled b-a-t-t-i-e. her family is
from mississippi. my grandfather's name is frank battie. his father, my
great grandfather, is named george battie.

in 1850, during the US census, they did not list a person's property, just
the names of slave owners and the count of the slaves. in mississippi,
there was a woman by the name of elizabeth beaty, spelled b-e-a-t-y, who
owned over fifty slaves. and i wonder if this is the cotton plantation my
family   roots   grew from. i wonder if this is the name my ancestors
placed aside their papers and fled   the   plantation   with. is
there a magnolia tree down in panola, mississippi, that has all of my fam-
ily's blood?

williams is the most common last name for black folks. after williams
there is johnson. then

smith

        jones

        brown

        jackson
racial traumas and triggers are formal greeting when   we   call
our oppressor's   name to   introduce   ourselves,
when   names   are   a   historical   leash.
          every   time   i meet a black person with the last name
battie, i wonder if we are finally attending the family reunion. every   time

i meet a white person with the last name battie, i wonder if they know what their family has done, what abuse has allotted their breath.

what a privilege to know which end of the whopping whip has your name on it, to know exactly what your name is attached to, to have a name embroidered on a bedroom door instead of the quarters. what a privilege, on the job application, at the airport, at the bank, in the emergency room.

and people wonder about black names: whythenamesaren'tshorter, why the r u n a w a y syllables aren't easier to catch, why our names chime like music when they traverse between lobes, about why we name our children after birds, after cars, after movement, wonder why our names are spelled with distinction, why black names always have a flair.

countries who declare independence get to name themselves. niggas will always know reclamation. and when the names do not have your lineage, when our names are not what you expect, then what did you expect? for us to introduce ourselves, still running, to shake hands still dripping

blood   you   drew?

A BRIEF ANECDOTE ON WHY WHITE PEOPLE STOPPED SAYING NIGG—

they aren't as common as a cotton plant in the antebellum south,
but you still see them.

every couple mundane suburban street roads you'd ride,
you were likely to smell the plaque peeling away at the air
more often than you'd see a crack.

that's what we called them,
in part because of the history,
mostly for the infinite sound they made.

the noise would crawl from the violet rubble of their mouths like a maimed
corpse fleeing its grave.

their bodies were hunched like sunflowers, bent for rotting.
their necks held maroon scars noosed round them as branding.
their tongues, brown and discolored, lay limp and ejected from their mouths,
a swollen ringed knot in the center.

once white folks had seen the bewitching for themselves,
                how the tongue nearly ripped into itself,
                how the tension made blood pool in the center of the flesh,
they figured they wouldn't say it any mo.'
didn't want to walk around with a genocide glistening between their lips.

the first hexing left a man mangled at a dinner table in front of his daughter,
said he kept pointing to the tv yelling on and on about the [   ],
                said he said the word
                he wasn't supposed
to have said
at least a dozen times that breath   until   it   caught,

until   it   began   to   swell   his   cheeks   like   a   tumor,

until his tongue bloomed into a chokehold
and he fell out
and changed colors
and his daughter

                                     stand

                                                                 screaming
the floor, now a basin brimmed with the copper foam pouring from a slit in
                                his   mouth

THE MUSE FOR THIS BLACK DYKE IS A DEAD WHITE MAN

I.

a harvard educated writer -- of course -- i am to build something immaculate -- from the dust of his breath -- not striking a thought -- but extracting a whimper -- makes me think on other happenings that don't spark attention -- due to a lack of cultural compatibility like standardized tests -- water polo or skiing -- camping and casserole

II.

t. s. eliot's the hollow men closes with a chorus -- *this is the way the world ends -- not with a bang but a wimper* -- a group of men straw stuffed perched on a gate during purgatory -- men sit on a wall with all the indifference they cared not to muster -- eyes stare still in witness to the death of others -- the men don't do -- the men don't say

III.

i imagine what i thought to be loud and has been devastatingly silent -- bad sex with no orgasms -- gaslighting and subtle strings -- which then made me think of my own heart -- of all the relationships that have bloomed and wilted at the center -- i thought of masculinity as huff and puff and whimper -- i thought of dying a slow death -- of scalpels and pipelines -- of stealthy silent ways they try to kill folks of color -- but then -- i thought -- i couldn't write about that stuff -- that stuff is a little too dark (get it) why be morbid on a sunny grave -- why talk about black death as though black death is not redundant enough already (get it) how black is to death as death is to dead (get it) get the wake -- get the certificate -- get it be it with a bang or a diagnosis

IV.

despite our incompatibility -- i know the hollow men eliot speaks of -- men who are bystanders to others' ill fate -- i call them allies -- men can stomach murder because they are not the ones dying -- that's the sorrow with hollow men -- watch a faggot burn cause they are not -- laugh at the joke so long as a mouth isn't opening toward them -- let a white waitress touch the black friend's hair -- talk about trans rights -- not about ending trans death -- this is the way the world ends -- this is the way the world ends

V.

what will we do with all this black black -- or all this death death -- or all the black death -- all the dead bodies left -- what will we do with all the hollowed we carry -- the carcasses of little black children puffed with straw -- imagine dark bodies stuffed -- preserved -- strung -- out -- on -- a -- wall -- a border -- in a museum -- spectators -- like myself -- look in the eyes of the dead -- and see a still reflection of what the dead saw last -- their death (get it) how seeing yourself in the dead makes you a witness -- at your own wake -- (get the wake) how death is to black as i am to black how i am to death (see) the irony -- in how dark i am -- how with only a whimper -- a white man's immaculacy yields my breath into dust

WATER

in 2010, six black teenagers drowned in the louisiana red river. researchers found that seventy percent of black people do not know how to swim and that blacks are three times more likely to drown. the question became: why do blacks possess a fear of water?

i've heard sharks followed slave ships crossing the atlantic ocean trailing black bodies thrown overboard.

i've heard during slave times, white masters refused to let blacks learn them to swim cause a swimming slave could get away, could swim to freedom, could figure out a way to wade in the water.

i've heard lil black kids ain't nothing but gator bait. gator bait let you catch an alligator so big, so vicious it bite like racism. black mamas be like, *keep your kids out the water, it ain't safe, chile.*

i heard a jim crow north and a ku kluxed south kept coloreds outta public swimming pools and off public water fountains. i heard

they hosed niggers down with a firefighter water hose how you hose down a rabid dog in the summertime heat of new orleans.

i heard, come hell or high water, they were gonna watch blax drown in a
                            hurricane down south,

heard they knew the levees was gonna give in and break, knew the waters was
                            coming to wash away.
tell me.
how do a nigger keep
they head above waters
if niggers can't swim?

niggas   can't doggie-paddle
niggas   can't tread water
niggas   jump, but never jump   in

{i sprint, you swim}

niggas   can't float our bodies,

too dense. we don't do with rain cause our hair *just got did.* i heard yes-
terday in detroit, they cut the water off. the water don't run. the faucets
run dry. kids are dehydrated {niggas is thirsty}.

heard they been gasping for air, been drowning in oppression for what
feels like forever. ever since crossing the atlantic: been feeling lost at
sea, been feeling like a fish   out   of   water, like a body
sinking
in the
deep
end, like treading troubled
waters

and drowning.

LOOK AT WHAT I'VE DONE!

i plant myself on my porch to smoke
a cigarette—a blade of fountain
grass brushes my leg so i grab it from
its roots &

         i kill it.

                a fruit fly dances a jig in front my glasses
                while i read in bed so i space my hands-
                apart & slap them closed &

i kill it.

for breakfast i add the coarse
salt-fresh garlic to the pan—
i saute the spinach &
i kill it.

i purchase live crab for the creole quiche
i bring to the pot luck—i place the shellfish
into the boiling water &   i kill it.

i reside in a building raised up from a
stolen forest & the birds—the deer—the
trees—all the slain ancestors stirring the clay,

                i have killed them.
white men

                timid of night
pulla pistol to the temple

of a thirteen year old black {   }
squeeze the
trigger &
this is   an errand   before   dinner.

ALADDIN'S GENIE ON EMANCIPATION

the first query from the stranger is

where are your shackles?

his eyes are bewildered
his mouth ajar
his question is a question
and i am still taken aback.

not the first time someone has mistaken me
for chattel. not the first time someone has been
unarmed by survival. over a century and my body
still knows not to belong to itself: to be another's
property, to call another person master. i want to
poof magic smoke   and fire and disappear.

but i am walking toward this stranger now
on wet cobblestone in a fleeting city. he calls

you have to grant me three wishes

he says genie
like he knows me
like he knows my name
genies don't have names
names are for the freed
he names me slave, says

*slave, do a trick
genie, grant a wish
tap dance, become a ship
or a bridge, put on a show
do jazz hands, shuck, smile,
jive, genie.*

aladdin granted me free, his very last request.
how he used the first two, kept me slave
long enough to get what he wanted. o, what

great privilege: to hope for someone else's
freedom and not have to be the angry bitch
to demand it. just cause you yearn you a bird
don't mean you can fly. don't make me liberated.
i can tell
the stranger
front of me
            wishes me
his slave
            wishes me
a dead thing
            wishes to

make sure
i do not wake
            wishes
me not to rise.
he looks me
in the eye, says

                                                            sing,

genie.

i stare.
place.   one.   foot.   front.   of the
other.
and i say

                    i wish i knew how it would feel to be free.

THE ELECTRIC SLIDE IS NOT A DANCE, MAN!

I wanna privy you to a little secret. Come close now. Good. So what you need to know is the electric slide is not a dance. It's a transmission code. What I'm trying to tell you is every time I need to leave here, every time I need to get to a place that feels like my mama's cooking or my brother's cackle booming from soot, I sound the gathering. I bring out the trumpets and horns whenever I need to shake this crypt dust settling my bones. I turn my stereo up. Just the other day, so-and-so tells me he wants me to teach 'im the moves. Nigga, I can't teach style. Can't learn blood to pound to a drum pulse so slick it glide. So free it ain't. Can't teach 'im or nobody else who not from where we from what's innate. I mean, man, shit, there is a place I need to get to, a grin I need to spread, a quaking of my foundation ungrounded from laughter. The code's an impenetrable thing; how the slide is suave, how the count off for the take off is the dip low, the count out. The down swing recollects our plot of land on this earth. Picking a leg high, a knee raised, a turn to the left is the way we know to leave our massacre behind, man. The dance floor is a square padlock you can't crack. Each space we take there is meant for us to occupy. Each brethren is attached to our side, our fronts, our backs. This pattern is a shield against depression or hunger hanging out of someone's blue eyes. Our bodies arrange a constellation in memory of the boy who was slain with no indictment, for the guillotined girl who went forgotten, for the housing stacked like the gut of the ship, the dogs and the waters. The blast off happens in sync and our spirits rupture ceilings. We ritual. Sacred. Secret. Originators of a beat cascading. The electric slide is how we leave here, how we ascend. This kinship is how we get to a place named joy and go home. That's blood, history, man. Ain't no teaching that.

I AM NEITHER THE POEM, NOR THE WORDS, NOR THE LETTERS, NOR THE IMAGES THEY ELICIT

on the morning this is written, a brown hawk uses its beak to pierce a
blue jay on a light post in the street. the hawk carries the jay by its neck
and glides across the sky. the birds in nearby trees chirp a chorus of fright
or protest.

on the day of my arrest
i conjure my death in one
hundred distinct sightings

when the officer pulls us   like a nigga
over i try hard not to look

try hard not to look   like prey
i try not to ask
too many questions
where the answer is   baton

i plead the fifth
when the officer
pats me down
on the trunk
of the car &
calls me sir

i do not reach for something   soft to use as weapon

when state troopers fold me
in half and throw me
into the police truck
i do not disassociate
this bending from a coming of age

i do not unthink myself

when i am sitting on the bench in the jailhouse
and my hands are behind my back i tell myself
i am not face down i am sitting on a bench not
an electrical pole i tell myself my cheeks aren't
burning into linoleum or pressed into a boot print

i am on a bench i say
i am upright i say
i am conscious

count the four shadows perched
around me i don't know if the officers
are the hawk in this allegory but i do
know this story ends with the blue jay
dead when the fifth white male officer
attempts to make conversation   i tell a joke   i jingle my handcuffs
like a fat belly

                 jolly
                 with
                 laughter
                 i puff out
                 my feathers
                 i shuck
because i want to outlive this cage
when the officer takes my fingerprints & asks
me to shift right for the camera i smile i praise

the day they capture me [live] girl in a dead mug
shot i tell myself the holding cell in this small town
is not a graveyard for a black woman tonight

i say

                         i am not a passing ballad

not a bird with crescendo caught

between its beak

i say

    i am not to die at the end of this tale

i grin through the cop into the clock & i imagine myself painting a tattoo out of the cuts the cuff leaves in my wrist i imagine instead of my name being carved into an epitaph i hear it ringing out instead i imagine my wife will hear me tell this tale of a brush with a hawk over & over i guess that means i see myself as surviving maybe i am not the blue jay after all maybe i confused my splendor for plumage you know sometimes death feels like a culmination i think i've earned you know sometimes my body is a story i think i know the end to but maybe in this narrative i am the

                                sky

i defied an instrument that was built to use my hollow bones as fuel was lucky to escape the hunt maybe in this fiction i am horizon-expansive a long life lived a front porch a wooden chair rocking forth & back into a black sun the blue jay is dead the hawk is figment the sky is open & infinite

and just a tale i tell
to lessen
the weight

MY MOTHER is a drinking gourd she is a
runaway slave along a shore my mother is a
still river her folks from mississippi she bred
black south side of chicago in the seventies
my mother is great migration got a gambler
for a father and a rifle for a mother my moth-
er is associate's degree in early childhood
education is three credits short from a B.A.
is food stuck in vending machine my mother
still ain't got what she paid for is all curse-
out-the-clerk-at-the-cashier-counter is all *i*
guess y'all are gonna have to work something
out cause I'm not about to pay for that my
mother is the difference between ghetto and
hood is a rumor sale not a thrift store my
mother is a christian is church going is-leave-
church-early-don't-sing-in-the-choir- no-
more-cause-it-seem-shady-behind-the-pul
pit my mother is two jobs and an empty piggy
bank is section eight for retirement plan is
no savings account no trust fund no money
'til the fifteenth of the month my mother is
machete for speech is too sharp to be killed
or followed my mother is a blade in a back
pocket is loud joke in a juke bar *ha-ha* my
mother is an oxymoron is a homophobe with
a strap-on for a daughter my mother is a
strong black woman behind every
disappearing vanishing missing murdered
black man my mother is an open casket is
meant to hold bodies is a vacant lot next to
a boarded-up home my mother is home
is sanctuary is god my mother is how black
don't crack her spine don't bend my mother
is still my mother is a steel bullet a loaded
shotgun

waiting

PARABLE

some mornings i wake and i am most like my mother,
a wide mouth daring light to flicker before i shine.

other mornings i am like my father, a shadow cast black
as american soil and as frequently uprooted.

i don't often tell this story of the white mahogany tree who fell madly in love
with the sun. the day they met in a closed field and couldn't stop

giving to one another. the tree carved the sun a home
and the sun fetched light and warmth.

i do not tell this story often of the offspring they fashioned from love,
the boy-child both waving branch and wild breeze, the girl-child

both splendor and flame, of the feverish narrator who weaves this fable.
no. it is not often that I tell this story of the traffic stop and arrest,

of the pat down and immigration lawyer, of the vows and home

splintered.

beloved reader, at the end of this story, the tree never even gets to say
goodbye. darling listener, at the end of this tale, the sun refuses to bask

in its glow. once upon a time there was earth
and sky and white men declared them countries

and the white men said some trees should not receive shine from some suns,
and so my father was deported. i do not tell this story often of the place leaves

voyage to when god plans their fall,
why the stars set themselves on fire just so we may
follow, of where the river is running to,

nor of why the willows weep. i do not recount this memory,
oh wretched witness, of the laws that rule this land
with a steel hold, of the land that unearthed my family,
of the home palpable in memory, alone. some mornings

i wake and i am a burning mahogany. and what i mean is there are days I am
engulfed. other mornings i wake and i am most

like the horizon, a meeting of cosmos and clay, a stretching across of bodies.
beholder of this tale, do you see now

how anguish keeps me from speaking this story?
do you understand now where the sun whisks to

at night? why she whispers a song only the green know?
why the orchards all grow limbs reaching toward the sky?

ACKNOWLEDGEMENTS

Without my family, I am not. I want to thank my mother, Patricia and my father, Rasheed. I love you both so much. Gratitude to my sister Patrice and my brother Rasheed Jr. Makalia, Miguel, Mauriana, Emmette, Eamon, Eli, Elasha, Emoni. My extended family, here on earth, or otherwise. My aunts and uncles, my cousins who show. Thank you.

I am grateful to my heart, Crystal Valentine, for holding me in friendship, craft, awe, and love.

I extend my gratitude to the city of Boston, for the way in which it rang me tight in migration. To all the artists, friends, and family living here or whom I've met in the arms of this city: Shamara Rhodes, Claudia Wilson, Golden, Oompa, Zenaida Peterson, Ashley Davis, Sam Rush, Angelica Maria, Janae Johnson, Jonathan Mendoza, Melissa Lozada-Oliva, Erich Haygun, Brandon Melendez, Tatiana Johnson, JR. Mahung, Marshall Gilson, Hewan Kassa, Sam Chin, Tope Sholola, Kofi Dadzie, Michelle Garcia, Andrine Pierriesaint, Agnes Ugoji, Anita Dias, Chinma Okananwa, Adonis Woods, Aisha Ramos, Demetrius Tolbert, Julissa Emile, Thomas Johnston, Amanda Torres, Kara Elliot-Ortega, Emil Eastman, Anthony Febo, Simone Beaubien, Tyanna Simmons, Lissa Piercy, Princess Moon, Alex Charamlabidies, Jha D., Bing Bodrick, Phree, Ricky Orng, D. Ruff, Sublime, Kaleigh O' Keefe, The House Slam, Daniel Tobin, John Skolyes, Kemi Alabi, Nicole Herring, Teresa Reiko Perales, Amanda Cheung.

I owe so much to Dr. Ruth Nicole Brown and Solhot, Molly Myers, Danez Smith, Ebony Stewart, Eve L. Ewing, Mahogany Brown, Elizabeth Acevedo, Clint Smith, Hieu Minh Nguyen, Franny Choi, Justice Ameer, Charlotte Abotsi, Chrysanthemum Tran, Jamila Woods, Muggs Fogarty, Hanif Abdurraqib, Siarra Freeman, Suzi Q. Smith, Desiree Delegaicomo, Paul Tran, Sherrie Zantea, Hadiza Mohammed, Camille Love, Matthew Akoto, Liane Hypolite, Debbie Sim, Jianan Shi, Jabari Asim.

I extend my gratitude to my editors, Emmanuel Oppong-Yeboah and Safia Elhillo. Thank you for being the first to see me, through this work.

Institutions and organizations who've provided me with muse or resource: The Haley House Bakery & Cafe, Emerson MFA Program, The Boston Foundation, Create Well Grant, The Isabella Stewart Gardner Museum, Arts and Business Council, Button Poetry, Codman Academy, MassLEAP.

Thank you to the journals who gave the first version of these poems a home:

Wus Good Magazine, *Tangled aka Rapunzel aka Long-Hair-Don't-Care And What*

Redivider Journal, *"Listen: My Right Hand is Covered in Blood", "Had My Parents Not Been Separated After My Father's Traffic Stop, Arrest, and Deportation from The United States of America,"* and *" Twerk Villanelle."*

ABOUT THE AUTHOR

Porsha Olayiwola is a writer, performer, educator and curator who uses afro-futurism and surrealism to examine historical and current issues in the Black, woman, and queer diasporas. She is an Individual World Poetry Slam Champion and is the current poet laureate for the city of Boston.

OTHER BOOKS BY BUTTON POETRY

If you enjoyed this book, please consider checking out some of our others, below. Readers like you allow us to keep broadcasting and publishing. Thank you!

Neil Hilborn, *Our Numbered Days*
Hanif Abdurraqib, *The Crown Ain't Worth Much*
Olivia Gatwood, *New American Best Friend*
Donte Collins, *Autopsy*
Melissa Lozada-Oliva, *peluda*
Sabrina Benaim, *Depression & Other Magic Tricks*
William Evans, *Still Can't Do My Daughter's Hair*
Rudy Francisco, *Helium*
Guante, *A Love Song, A Death Rattle, A Battle Cry*
Rachel Wiley, *Nothing Is Okay*
Neil Hilborn, *The Future*
Phil Kaye, *Date & Time*
Andrea Gibson, *Lord of the Butterflies*
Blythe Baird, *If My Body Could Speak*
Desireé Dallagiacomo, *SINK*
Dave Harris, *Patricide*
Michael Lee, *The Only Worlds We Know*
Raych Jackson, *Even the Saints Audition*
Brenna Twohy, *Swallowtail*

Available at buttonpoetry.com/shop and more!